ALL AROUND THE WORLD
LATVIA

by Kristine Spanier, MLIS

Ideas for Parents and Teachers

Pogo Books let children practice reading informational text while introducing them to nonfiction features such as headings, labels, sidebars, maps, and diagrams, as well as a table of contents, glossary, and index.

Carefully leveled text with a strong photo match offers early fluent readers the support they need to succeed.

Before Reading

- "Walk" through the book and point out the various nonfiction features. Ask the student what purpose each feature serves.
- Look at the glossary together. Read and discuss the words.

Read the Book

- Have the child read the book independently.
- Invite him or her to list questions that arise from reading.

After Reading

- Discuss the child's questions. Talk about how he or she might find answers to those questions.
- Prompt the child to think more. Ask: Forming a human chain is one form of peaceful protesting. What are other examples of peaceful protesting?

Pogo Books are published by Jump!
5357 Penn Avenue South
Minneapolis, MN 55419
www.jumplibrary.com

Copyright © 2023 Jump!
International copyright reserved in all countries.
No part of this book may be reproduced in any form without written permission from the publisher.

Library of Congress Cataloging-in-Publication Data

Names: Spanier, Kristine, author.
Title: Latvia / by Kristine Spanier, MLIS.
Description: Minneapolis, MN: Jump!, Inc., [2023]
Series: All around the world | Includes index.
Audience: Ages 7-10
Identifiers: LCCN 2022023598 (print)
LCCN 2022023599 (ebook)
ISBN 9798885242004 (hardcover)
ISBN 9798885242011 (paperback)
ISBN 9798885242028 (ebook)
Subjects: LCSH: Latvia—Juvenile literature.
Classification: LCC DK504.56 .S63 2022 (print)
LCC DK504.56 (ebook)
DDC 947.96—dc23/eng/20220519
LC record available at https://lccn.loc.gov/2022023598
LC ebook record available at https://lccn.loc.gov/2022023599

Editor: Jenna Gleisner
Designer: Molly Ballanger

Photo Credits: photovideoworld/Shutterstock, cover; Levranii/Shutterstock, 1; Pixfiction/Shutterstock, 3; LukaKikina/Shutterstock, 4; Greens and Blues/Shutterstock, 5; imantsu/iStock, 6-7; ErikKarits/iStock, 8-9tl; WildlifeWorld/Shutterstock, 8-9tr; Nadezda Murmakova/Shutterstock, 8-9bl; Batalina/iStock, 8-9br; ILMARS ZNOTINS/AFP/Getty, 10; Chamille White/Shutterstock, 11; REUTERS/Alamy, 12-13, 18-19; Gints Ivuskans/AFP/Getty, 14-15; freeskyline/Shutterstock, 16 (kotletes); Fanfo/Shutterstock, 16 (aukstā zupa); ronstik/Shutterstock, 16 (rye); Alexander Mychko/Dreamstime, 16 (rosols); Balakleypb/Shutterstock, 17; Harijs Pelle/Shutterstock, 20-21; RomanR/Shutterstock, 23.

Printed in the United States of America at Corporate Graphics in North Mankato, Minnesota.

TABLE OF CONTENTS

CHAPTER 1
A Lot of Water 4

CHAPTER 2
Protesting for Freedom 10

CHAPTER 3
Daily Life 16

QUICK FACTS & TOOLS
At a Glance 22
Glossary 23
Index 24
To Learn More 24

CHAPTER 1
A LOT OF WATER

Do you want to look for **amber**? You can find it along the Baltic Sea. Latvia has more than 300 miles (483 kilometers) of Baltic coastline. Welcome!

amber

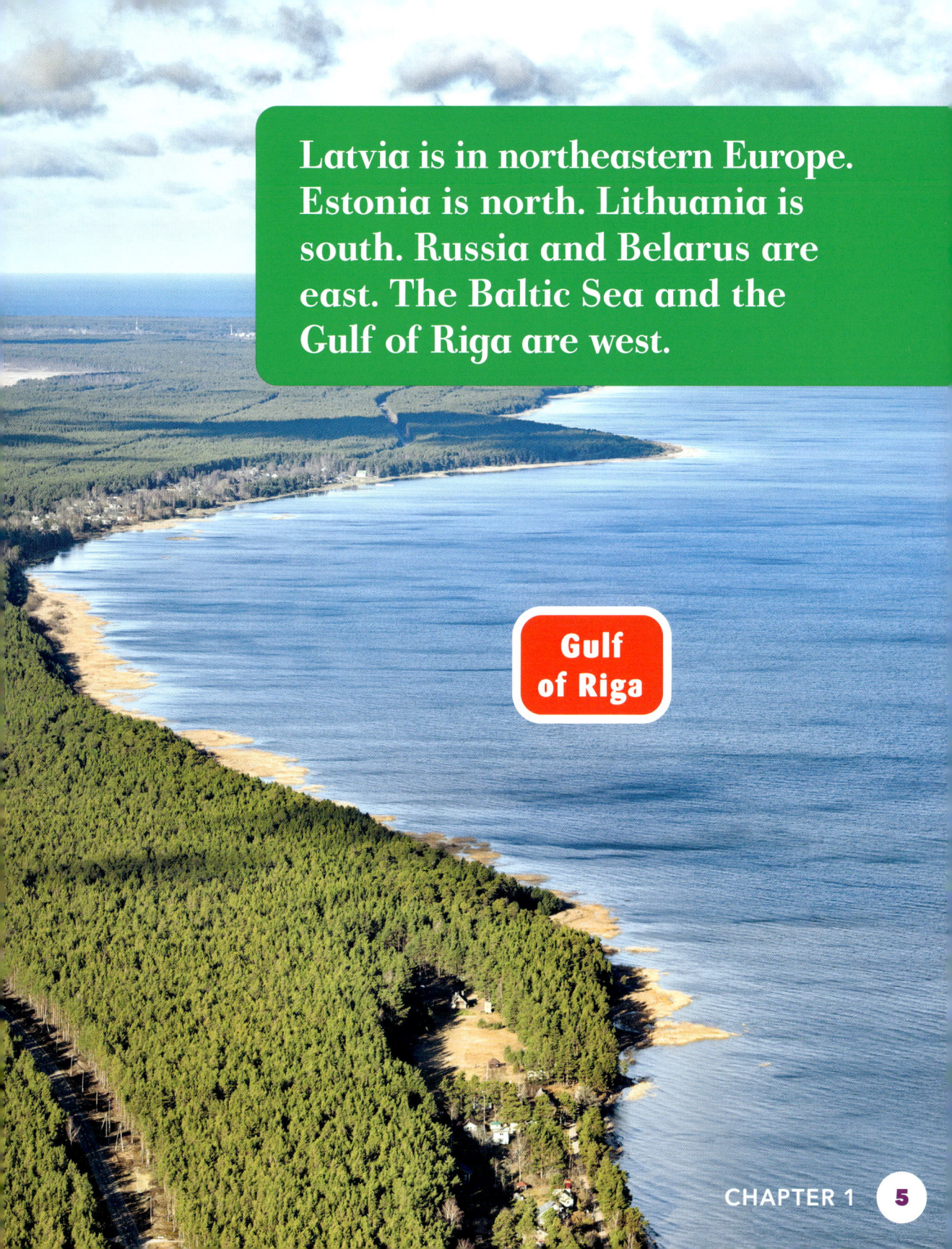

Latvia is in northeastern Europe. Estonia is north. Lithuania is south. Russia and Belarus are east. The Baltic Sea and the Gulf of Riga are west.

Gulf of Riga

CHAPTER 1

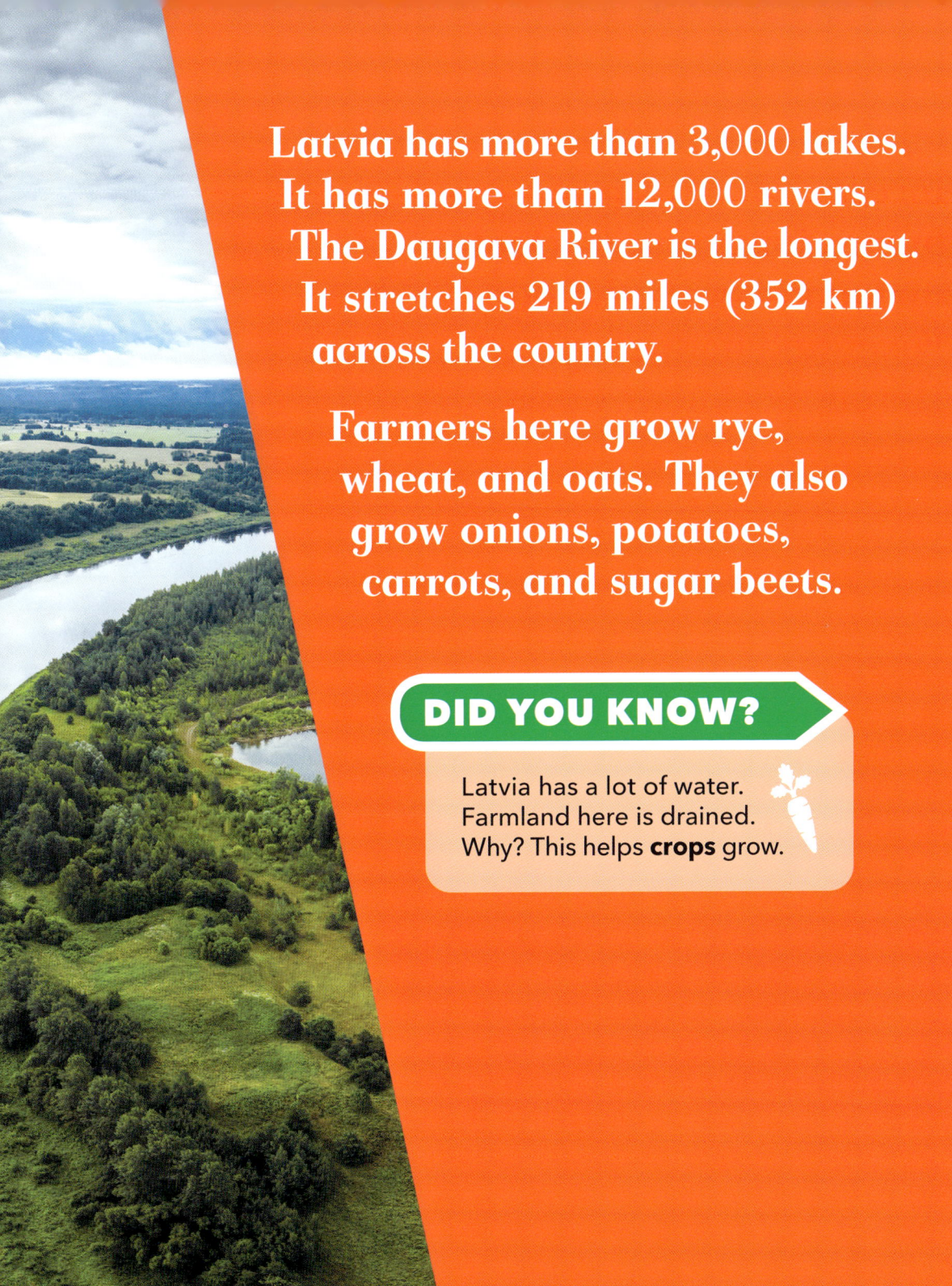

Latvia has more than 3,000 lakes. It has more than 12,000 rivers. The Daugava River is the longest. It stretches 219 miles (352 km) across the country.

Farmers here grow rye, wheat, and oats. They also grow onions, potatoes, carrots, and sugar beets.

DID YOU KNOW?

Latvia has a lot of water. Farmland here is drained. Why? This helps **crops** grow.

More than half of Latvia is forested. Forests make good homes for animals. Deer and moose walk the woods. Foxes and badgers prowl. Herons nest near water.

moose

fox

badger

heron

CHAPTER 1

CHAPTER 2
PROTESTING FOR FREEDOM

Latvians can vote when they turn 18. They **elect** the Saeima. This group of people makes laws. It also elects the president.

ballot

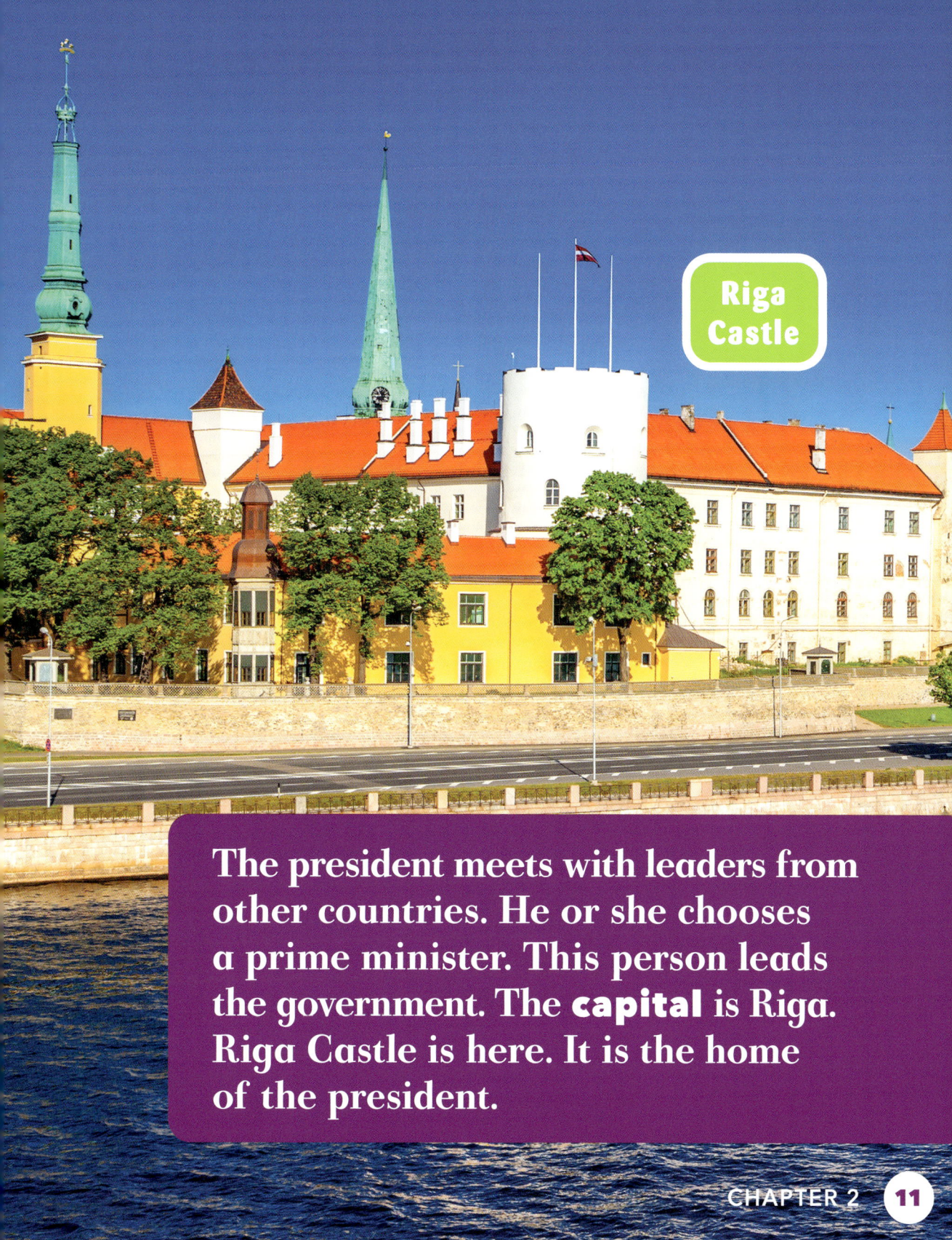

Riga Castle

The president meets with leaders from other countries. He or she chooses a prime minister. This person leads the government. The **capital** is Riga. Riga Castle is here. It is the home of the president.

1989 protest

The **Soviet Union** took control of Latvia in 1940. Latvians **protested**. They wanted freedom. In 1989, they formed a human chain. People from Estonia and Lithuania joined. Two million people stretched across the three countries! It was a peaceful protest. In 1991, all three countries became free.

TAKE A LOOK!

How long did it take Latvia to regain freedom? Take a look!

1940
The Soviet Union takes control of Latvia's government.

1993
A **democratic** government forms in Latvia.

1989
Latvia, Estonia, and Lithuania work together. The three countries peacefully protest.

1988
A group called the Latvian People's Front forms. They work for freedom.

1991
The Soviet Union breaks up. Latvia gains freedom.

CHAPTER 2

Latvia wanted to protect its freedom. In 2004, it joined two organizations to help. One is the **North Atlantic Treaty Organization (NATO)**. The other is the **European Union (EU)**. Countries in these groups work together. They work for peace.

WHAT DO YOU THINK?

Cooperating helps people reach their goals. Do you think countries should work together? Why or why not?

CHAPTER 2

CHAPTER 3
DAILY LIFE

The biggest meal of the day here is dinner. It starts with soup. Aukstā zupa is served cold. Kotletes are meat patties. A tasty side dish is rosols. It is a potato salad. Rye bread goes with many meals.

kotletes

aukstā zupa

rosols

sap

People in Latvia **tap** birch trees. Why? They collect the **sap**. They make it into a sweet drink.

CHAPTER 3

Most students here learn English. They attend school until at least ninth grade. Then they can choose a secondary school. Some schools prepare students for jobs. Others get them ready for college.

CHAPTER 3

Would you like to go to a song and dance festival? One is in Riga every five years. More than 40,000 children from across the country go! Parades take place all week. So do activities. It is a way to celebrate Latvian **heritage**.

Latvia is fun! Do you want to visit?

WHAT DO YOU THINK?

In the years between the festival, children practice. They participate in contests to earn spots at the festival. Do you think this is fair? Why or why not?

CHAPTER 3   21

QUICK FACTS & TOOLS

AT A GLANCE

LATVIA

Location: northeastern Europe

Size: 24,938 square miles (64,589 square kilometers)

Population: 1,842,226 (2022 estimate)

Capital: Riga

Type of Government: parliamentary republic

Languages: Latvian (official), Russian, Polish, Ukrainian, Belarusian

Exports: lumber, broadcasting equipment, wheat, medicines

Currency: euro

GLOSSARY

amber: A yellowish-brown substance that forms when tree sap fossilizes.

capital: A city where government leaders meet.

crops: Plants grown for food.

democratic: A form of government in which the people choose their leaders in elections.

elect: To choose someone by voting for him or her.

European Union (EU): A group of European countries that have joined together to encourage economic and political cooperation.

heritage: Traditions and beliefs that a country or society considers an important part of its history.

North Atlantic Treaty Organization (NATO): An organization of countries that have agreed to give each other military help. This group includes the United States, Canada, and some countries in Europe.

protested: Demonstrated against something.

sap: The liquid that flows through a plant, carrying water and food from one part of the plant to another.

Soviet Union: A former country of 15 republics that included Russia, Ukraine, and other nations of eastern Europe and northern Asia.

tap: To make a hole in a tree to draw out a liquid.

Latvia's currency

INDEX

amber 4
animals 8
Baltic Sea 4, 5
crops 7
Daugava River 7
Estonia 5, 12, 13
European Union 15
festival 21
food 16
forests 8
freedom 12, 13, 15
government 11, 13
Gulf of Riga 5
heritage 21
lakes 7
Lithuania 5, 12, 13
North Atlantic Treaty Organization 15
protest 12, 13
Riga 11, 21
Riga Castle 11
rivers 7
Saeima 10
sap 17
Soviet Union 12, 13
students 18
vote 10

TO LEARN MORE

Finding more information is as easy as 1, 2, 3.
1. Go to www.factsurfer.com
2. Enter "Latvia" into the search box.
3. Choose your book to see a list of websites.